GOD
LEVEL

GOD LEVEL

LEVEL

KRATOS, EZUZIA & DUNAMIS

EMMANUEL AKAN OKON

ARPress
ILLUMINATING IDEAS
EMPOWERING VOICES

ARPress
45 Dan Road Suite 36
Canton MA 02021
Hotline: 1(888) 821-0229
Fax: 1(508) 545-7580

Ordering Information:
Quantity Sales. Special discounts are available on quantity purchases by corporations, associations, and others. For details, contact the publisher at the address above.

Printed in the United States of America.

ISBN-13   Paperback   979-8-89330-498-5
                 eBook   979-8-89330-499-2

Library of Congress Control Number: 2024901788

Table of Contents

APPRECIATION

I would like to appreciate God almighty for giving me the inspiration to do this.

The friend and members of God comes mission international. Bro Charles, Sir Pow Glaya sister Relisia and other faithful members and ministers of God all over the world. Members of full gospel businessmen fellowship which I am a member for 2-decade, other mentors like Bishop prophesy King in the United Kingdom and others too precious and too numerous to mentor.

Thank you and God bless.

INTRODUCTION

This book is coming to world at a time nobody expected it. This is compilation of many years of studies, pondering, meditation and reflection on a complicated topic as this one.

Despite people opinions and position, interpretation and postulation, God is God; Jesus is Jesus, and the holy spirit is who he is.

I will advise the reader to please sometime to come out of the misleading information so far about any of the characters:

1. - God
2. - Jesus
3. - The holy sprit

Help yourself if you are already a Christian, approach this book with an open mind. Take a pencil and paper and meticulously follow the bible passage and real for yourself. If you are not yet a believer or born again you need to with help of this book, give your life to Christ and become born again:

1. - Repent
2. - Be born again
3. - Be baptized in the holy spirit.

This is the set order, but God can make work the way he wants. But the essence of these is the unity in the faith.

Let us not leave human effort out of this equation. Human are used to witness to us before he become born again as pastors, prophets, and evangelist. No wonder Jesus prays let them be come as we are: United. Jn 19:

Read and read as many times as you can till you get it because your life depends on it enjoy your that they be conformed to the image of his dear son.

<u>Rom 8: 29:</u>

For those God for new he also predestined to be conformed

To the image of his son: that he might be the first born among Many brothers and sisters.

CHAPTER 1

THE GOD LEVEL

"God showed himself to be visible to us. God created us with the nature of God."

(A) INTRODUCTION

The God level is the highest in both heaven and earth, you have to understand how this realm operate if you don't learn to know who God is, his likeness or dislikes God is not

1. A mechanical Robot
2. Specific
3. Feeling
4. He has a mindset you too must have this kind of mindset to be on the same page with him.

Example: God loves praise, trumpet, shouting, dancing, God want truth.

It is important to have the knowledge of God both information and revelation.

We need to know God and know what he wants and give him people like the presence of God without knowing him in person presence – skill but the person of God needs more than skill but his personality, charter, and disposition.

Praise him on the how samely cymbal.

Also praise him on a high cymbal because everything is significant before God.

- Know when to talk and the time to be quiet
- There are things you do, and they don't do.
- Don't touch the mountain or the people shouldn't touch it
- Things must be done holiness, done in certain way.
- Reverence is given to God when he appears.

- Jesus is more liberal in doing things chapter

(B) Two things to learn are written in his word of God.
1. The man who works with God must show discernment
2. Humility is a standard
3. You do only what he says not what you went
4. You must show deferment to Gods presence and instruction
5. God wants detail
6. Glory must be created by action- Give him everything he ask for

MINISTRYING TO THE LORD

Waiting upon the Lord requires knowing him and ready to know who the father is will give the expose about him.

CHAPTER 2

NATURE OF THE FATHER

Mt 4:46 – 48 VS 45

"That you may be the Children of your father.

Here we don't make choices of people we want to love and these we don't."

(A) Perfection = Maturity

- Righteousness, Holiness with maturity is not right.
- Maturity makes you perfect, holing real Righteous comes through growing in the faith.
- Corruption can come where there is no maturity.
- Perfection is good but it can lead you to been harsh, mean and judgmental.
- God goes all the way to do good for us irrespective of our present faith. He does not struggle to do us good whether we are sinners or righteous.
- God makes the sun to rise on both the just and unjust.
- To judge whether to help a sinner or not is preposterous.

Note Gods format is the rainbow. Love for everybody mature love is the greatest Jesus made the decision to die for the whole world. He did any, die for a section of the world. He died for everybody including the abietenes, civilized, uncivilized Jews white, black or Asians. All these don't matter, people make mistakes and there:

1. You are only as right as long as you become mature, more community base
2. Connection to world view and respect for differences.
3. Patient with other people
4. Allowing people to make mistakes and learn true inclusions.

(B) MATURITY AGE OF GODS IN MINISTRY

- 18 YRS - 20 YRS - 30 YRS
- Fulfillment of the people of God.
- God is a god of growth

God didn't make Adam a baby but full-grown man because God loves maturity. Adams maturity however didn't show because he didn't have the childhood.

However, Jesus had the childhood and grew in his sufferings.

Galatians 4: 1 – 2

Now I say the heir as long as he is a child differ from nothing as long servant…

(C) Maturity is moving on to the next higher dimension.

- Growth is about moving from Child – Adolescent - Maturity or Puberty – full grown person.
- The whole of the fivefold ministry are servants gifts they moved from Gods servants to become friends of Jesus.
- Darkness – In God
- When we see dark, things happen we don't see
- Samuel – I will dwell in your thick darkness.
- Jesus told the lew – this is your time of darkness

(B1) Maturity stage

Friends of God

We can get more done as a friend than a servant. A son as long as he is a child - Inexperience no skill full. When we begin to move away from that servant hood mentality you cannot

1. Know the secrets of your master
2. You cannot relate with the master and these things he cannot share the whole thing with servants.

Your moving out of childhood helps to move up or grow up with God. We should be doing to the word not just listeners only – That is maturity the work of ministry is the free fold ministry to get us to maturity.

4

CHAPTER 3

THE FINE FOLD MINISTRY

(A) WHAT IS THE FATHER LIKE

1. Mature - He promotes materially
2. He does not promote staying in childishness, adol the seral
3. He send

(B) WHAT PROMOTES OUR GROWTH.

If you are mature and grow in the faith when Jesus will come and introduce you to the father.

Mt 11: 25,26,27

TRAINING WHEELS – Initial process father

Mt 11: 27

All things are delivered to me by the father…….

1. It doesn't just happen when you are born again
2. They tell us about the father, you are to meet with the father when you get matured. You should know about the part of taton – c or training.

1. Adam didn't accept Jesus as a training wheel
2. Adam fell and refused Jesus at the garden of Eden

(C) WHAT HINDERS OUR GROWTH

He that received me, received you.

Is Jesus and God (are) the same?

Jn 17:
Eternal life is not only to know about Jesus but also to know about God and the holy spirit.

Jn 14: 28
Jesus said my father is greater than I
I am going to my father for my father is greater than I.

Jn 10: 27 – 29
My father is greater than all. Nobody can pluck them away from me

Jesus will hand over power of God

1 Car 15: 24 – 28
God the father put all things under is feet.

Vs 27
The father is greater than Jesus

Vs 28
The son will be subject to God

Jn 17: 1 – 3
The only true God

And Jesus whom you have sent

Jn 16: 27
They are now friends of Jesus.

Vs 23
In that day you will not ask me anything but whatever

Vs 25
Proverbs not but show planning

Vs 26
At that day of maturity – I don't pay for you but the father himself with you.......

Jesus at this stage does not moropolise the relationship with God but you and God has direct contact now. God recognized you and can listen to you directly.

CHAPTER 4

GOD HEAD

1. God the father
2. Jesus
3. Holy sprit

The Christian faith is for Us to explore: We need to be renewed because our mind died a long time ago.

Eph 2: 1

Majority of our brain died due to sin.

1. Adam brains died
2. Adam sprit died

Eph 2: 1

We are quickened our spirit.

Eph 4: 23

Be renewed in the spirit of your mind.

Quickened in the spirit

1. God love is always committed to live
2. No other
3. God is love – Love of life

Sin killed our brain our sprit and soul when they ate the wrong Fruit – The fruit of darkness is the devil wants to get your mind so he can stop you.

The blood of Jesus helps us – When Jorah comes, we reconnect to who we ought to be. It becomes instant, mature, and good to go.

(A) Moses splits the sea by the fathers assist

Moses splitted the red sea by the instruction of God and when he did what God said: It became apparent. The red sea handled perfectly.

7

Walk before me and be this perfect

When you get to the father all you desire need not traing or retain to get going but it happens perfectly.

He does all things well.

(B) Our God percentage
- 100% - of God
- 1-90% - Incomplete
- 2-80% - Incomplete

How To be God this level
1. Only ask
2. Have faith in the father – God
3. You got understand who God is his become he does the. The extra –ordinary

(C) WHO DID IT
1. Moses did all these by the word
2. Jesus did all these by his word
3. Commanded a tree to die physically not symbolically
4. Moses set frogs, open the earth – The 10 plagues etc.
5. If your things with your mouth it must be with your mind.

Rom 10.

Sin kills our brain on spirit and soul when they ate the wrong Fruit – The Fruit of darkness is death.

The devil wants to get your mind so he can stop you.

The blood of Jesus helps us – When Jorah comes, we reconnect to who we ought to be. It becomes instant, mature, and good to go.

Moses splitted the red sea by the instruction of God and when he did what God said: It become apparent – The red sea hudel perfectly.

Walk before me and be those perfect - When you get to the father all your desire need not training or retany to get going but it happens perfectly.

He does all things well.

You must intune your mind with your mouth so "When you get connected with the father, he tells you his original plan."

We are Kings and Queens.

CHAPTER 5

GOD MAN – WE ARE GOD

GOD level What we are taught we are though to know only God as a person, but God is an office.

Jnsah 82: 6

- Prince of the world
- God of this world
- Adams was the prince of this world and God of the world

Gods DNA

The fullness of us is the God of this
PS1. His staff and God comfort me

(A) MOSES as God

Moses you will be like a God to Pharoah and Aana would be like you.

Moses was promoted to the God rcahm

1 - Power over water

God divided the water over the fimament. So, God allowed Moses to split the water. He divided oceans and waters and rivers, the salt sea, the tubutaines, waterfalls anddmelol even the well in our backyard.

Gen 1: 6 – 7

God the father splited the water in the sky and that beneath the sky.

Exo 14:

God divided the fimenent and also instructed Moses to divide the sea like a God.

1. Jesus turned water to wine
   - Refresh the people

- Anointing and glory
- Kingdom
- Power
- Glory

We are Gods. We are the image and likeness of God

(B) PROPHETS WHO BECAME GOD

1. EXO 4: 14 - MOSES EXAMPLE
2. Godship is not just a person but also an office

(A) Lucifer wanted to get the God realm 100% like US but couldn't have it

(B) The God level is that which humbles and stay under God, but Lucifer and all the demons collectively want to use up the discretion of God but: rather want to operate in the realm of God. That is not his job.

(C) God tille takes over the whole world - you move from the position you are now to another position - We call the shot here.

(C) DARK PRINCE – Lucifer claimed to be a God because he stole it from Adam

Lucifer is a dark prince. What he did is his prince, but he is crazy.

1. We don't need to dishonor him
2. We don't dishonor all other angels
3. But we don't allow them to talk trash
4. All that he was is just nasty and totally acceptable
5. What he used to be is no longer true. He has been stuppes of all he used to be
6. Jesus gave us all he lost to the devil
7. Satan fell - failed and is still falling everyday

DEATH
1. 1st DEATH
2. 2nd SECOND DEATH.

The kingdom of God is growing brighter and brighter every day, but the kingdom of darkness is falling and becoming darker and darker everyday, every second, every hour, and every minutes.

TOPIC of God Level
1. Secret place
2. Shadow of the almighty
3. Peter when he receives the keys to the kingdom, He started to operate in God realm
4. Shadow protects you for heit – offencer
5. God is perfect
6. The place in churls

Note
- Secret place of God
- What benefits at the secret place and his presence

Note
- Isaiah saw his hand
- Moses saw his back pant
- We saw His CROSS - What did the cross do to you.
- Moses couldn't see his face SK Jesus hadn't come but saw his back.

(D) SOMETHING IS WRONG.

What is wrong -

1. Born again experience
2. Experience of meeting with the father

1. Jesus paid the price for us to meet with the father
2. Jesus spoke so much about the father - when do we acknowledge
3. Redemption of Jesus program is to meet the father
4. The love of the father
5. All the cute things we learnt about the father is to meet up with him

6. All the scripline inceated on attention to the father.

DESCRIPTION OF GOD THE FATHER

1. Ezekiel – description of
2. Moses and his
3. Elijah

CHAPTER 6

(A) Quickened By God

1. <u>THE father</u>

   A) Our mind
   B) Our brain
   C) Our sprit
   D) Our everything
   E) Our blood
   F) Our smews, Ea2ymes
   G) Our DNA

<u>SIGNAL</u>

- Ezekiel – Fire whist top and fire waist down
- Moses in Sinai

(B) 21ST Century Christian

1. Don't meant to see God face to face because I like the old Jews. I am okay with the Jesus
2. The

As many as received him to the he gave power – Ye shall become powerful after the holy sprit.

- Jesus gave us excuse
- Holy spirit - Dima mis
- The father gave us Dominion
- God gave us authority
  1. Holy spirit a gift
  2. Jesus fivefold ministry
  3. Father gives us everything Dominion

KINGDOM REPRESENTATION
1. Express image

If you don't believe in the one greater than Jesus, how are you going to do geater looks. Because I go to my father.

My mission is to reconale you to someone greater then, me God sits with God and acknowledges the father is greater than himself.

HEAD SHIP OF GOD
The head of Jesus in God.
The Head of man is Jesus, and the Head of woman is man.

HOOK UP TO GOD
We must connect with the 3 person of God

1. Father
2. Son
3. And the holy ghost.

Jude - Earnest continual the faith that was

THE NEW BREED
1. Jesus came to connect us with the father

2. The one jean died for us to meet

3. The one that compelled Jesus to submit totally to his will

DIFFERENCE IN MIRACLES
1. Miracles with the father. Dominion – over moon $ sm and constellation – Domneon over the first who rules over water. Joshua had dominion over time Ps & word of knowledge creators.
2. Miracles with the Holy ghost
3. Miracles of with Jesus.

Jesus is a gift of the father The Holy sprit is also a gift from the father.

God is giving us dominion over the things that control staff.

Example: One rule territory don't send, because we are made out of it.

The fish Jesus says to Peter go and get "COIN" and pay our tax.

He knows where to get payment from.

Jn 14:

She said my relationship with you will start with me and you will start with me and you but will end with the father.

Gods desire is not to make us just apostles, prophets and evargelist but to make us Gods.

NOT BY TITLES

1. bishop
2. Priest
3. Bishops
4. Archbishops

Not by clothes and by Names and nomen clehoic

The earnest expectation of the creature is the manifaction of the sons of God.

Sons - sons run the show

Jn 14:

We have been Duped – Morning with father - walking with CRATOS.

When we walk with the father we start to walk in the god level - He makes you into a jnr god level – This is were we do the extra ordinary stuff like him

Adam

Lost his glory and gave up his title but Jesus gave us the god level.

Death reign from Adam – Moses

Here was dispute over the body of Moses – God buried Moses because Moses was a God not just a prophet.

God of gods.

1. Jesus
2. Moses
3. Ehjah
4. We – You and I

(C) THREE VOICES IN 3 Person and one

Who do men say I am

God spoke through Peter and gave a rerelation of Jesus.

1. Anything Jesus is glorified - The holy spirit is glorifying him
2. God also glorify Jesus
3. The father also is a sprit
4. All 3talk about all of them and themselves

The father was in Christ reconciling the world to himself.

CREATION MYSTERIES

Gen 1
1. Let there be light – five
2. Let firmament chute the water – Atmosphere and water sphere space
   A - Moses split the red sea.
   B - Elijah & Esha split the river
3. Let the firmament divide the earth.
   A - God caused the east wind
   B - By the blast of his nosfils he spited the sea

God breaths into our nostril and we came alive and without air and oxygen we die.

Every day we live

Exe: prophecy to the wind – WHAT GOD USE IN CREATION the, Hebrews understood, it is the breath of of God

1. Breath of God
2. Hand of God
3. Finger of God
4. Angels of God
5. Jesus' power
6. Us – as collaborators or workers with God

WHY GOD USES WATER/OXYGEN

1. Wind – holy ghost
2. Holy spirit is transferred though:

A - Speaking

B - Wind

C - Laying up of hands

There is atmosphere and threw is no land – but God said let the landmass come out of the sea.

By the power of God, the whole world came out of deluge. The world came out of the water including humans because humans were made out of dirt.

(D) GROWTH IN MAN

God knew we will have powers like him. Like a child. A child has all the things complete example A girl

1. She has womb
2. She has vagina
3. She is a woman

But she will grow into it if he is a male child.

1. He has penis.
2. He has sperm
3. He has everything a man is supposed to have
4. He has brain to grow

But he must grow up to that point.

REVELATION OF WHO JESUS IS AND THEIR POSITION OF GOD.

1. All things are not possible with me.
2. The father sent me.
3. 1 cor 15 all power has been given to me excluding the power of the father.
4. Jesus told the 2 sons of Zebedee. It is not for meto give who swifs on left and right of the throw, but the faith does that
5. Jesus said '' I don't know when the judgment will come.

(E) USING YOUR MIND – Brain.

1. Dead brain comes back alive 100% of the brain will be restored.
2. The heart is dead – No love no feeling.

The heart felt loving prayer of a righteous mind availed much - Cos wonderful things are done. Unto him that is able to exceedingly abundant above all. - Eph 3:

John 14: 21 - 23

VS 23 – The father himself will love him and we will come to him. When you start loving Jesus, he prepares you and start coming to you together with the father

Jn 14: 28

You can't know Jesus except the father shows him and send him and you cannot know the father except Jesus reveals him and you receive the holy spirit except Jesus sends him. The three are united. " CRATOS POWER"

HOW TO BECOME A GOD

1. Dreams – Thomas Edison Martin Luther King'
2. Vision.

CHAPTER 7

WHO I AM

1 My Calling – My Identity
1. Who are you?
2. Why are you here

(A) Inheritance by line or ancestry

Jn 1: 19 – Priest and Levites asked what Linage John came from Record of John ancestory physically, spiritually, financially and emolirally.

(B) Maxima says who you are

1. VS 20 I am not the Christ.
2. VS 21 what there are you Ehjah – Malachi propleg of another Elijah
3. Mt 11: 17 – 15 John was VS 12 – Elijah but he didn't VS 14 Knew it.
4. You can receive this revalation this is the Elijah to come - John didn't know who he was
5. John 1: 23 – He said I am, I am the voice of an speaking in the wilderness_____

God will give you the work of whom you ought to be but does not reveal everything b/c prophecy is in pent. But your lineage or amestry would tell you who you are

Jn 11: 21

Who are thou –

Who are you – what is your purpose on earth and what you should preach.

MINISTRY STYLES

1. Kathnym Colemans Ministry

2. Oral Robert – Lay hands of people
3. Kemeth Hajni
4. Leslice Sumrall

God will let you taste his glory, enjoy his glory, eat his glory but don't take that glory to yourself. Similar identity with people who had come before you like God told me. Your ministry is like that of postle Paul. Learn about Paul and you will learn a lot from him. I am stralying of Paul when Jesus came to me and said to me now learn of me. Paul did not tell us of how to become:

1. Be like God.
2. Command the respect of God.
3. Paul didn't teach us to be in the same image and likeness of God.

So Paul taught me the introductory partern of God. All this decided to build relation with God.

CHAPTER 8

WHERE IS GODS' MIRACLE

I ask these questions all the time where we are now. We want to see Gods glory.

THE NEED OF ACKNOWLEDGE THE FATHERS AND STUDY THEM

The men and women used the past heard specific information and secret of God. Men God People used had spiritual connection. Men are attached to Mentors e.g.,

Jesus - John - Baptism
Jesus - Moses -
David - David -

Moses
12 - Spies
70 - Elders
120 - Elders

Attacked to be killed
Moses
Jesus

JOHNS LINEAGE WAS LINKED TO ELIJAH

1. Rebuke the king – ran
2. Elijah – John rebuke iterod for marrying his brother's wife.

Joshua - careful mom/son
Elijah - Elisha
Elisjha - Gehazy
Eph 1: 17

1. Hope of you calling in Christ Jesus Future -
2. And the riches of the glory in the inheritance in the saint's 3rd dimension is the level of glory.

God is coming for a glowers church. In 1 Suh 61 – the glory of God shall be seen in us

<u>Darkness Irrespective.</u>

1. We will shine
2. We will arise
3. Darkness will not run us out of the town.
4. The glory of God will be seen

<u>Definition of glory:</u>

1. The face of God – Himself The knowledge of knowledge of God is seen in the face of Jesus the glory is God – church
2. The glory is a replica of God. The amounting is alun God is with us. Our glory is we walking with God. Glory of God is the fullmest of who he is "Before, now and to come."

The riches of the glory of his inheritance in the saint.

1. Finances - level to level
2. Love - level to level

Riches can be immediate because I have an inheritance – Standing on the finished look Vs 19 - What is the exceeding power ------ above principally and power.

<u>WHAT WE HAVE FROM GOD.</u>

1. Hope
2. Inheritance
3. Exceeding greatness of his power

What is the exceeding greater of his power towards is vand.

According to his working power in us - Power - KRATOS

Holy ghost - Dunamis

Jn 1: - Jesus - Dynamite – Ezuzia, Gave them power over unclean sprit

EZUZIA - Exceeding power – Jesus was raised from the dead by KRATOS + DUMAMIS

NEW SPECHES

Father + Holy combined raised Jesus – God is doing exceeding greater dimension in the days. The earnest expectation of the people of the world.

(A) RAISING THE DEAD

Bedrock for explanation.
1. Ezuzia + Dunamis + Kartos
2. Jesus + Holy + Power = God

When the father raises the dead, it's different from how the holy spirit does and how Jesus do.

3 days Limit for raising the dead: People avoid people dead after 3 days even medically, in the medical world – But with Kratos: Bum and fluid. But Ezekiel: Can these dead bones live.

People who raise the dead in Old Testament.
1. Elijah
2. Elisha

Reclation:

Elisha – dead for over 10 yrs and when a soldier was thrown at him. He got up. Ezekiel raises a whole army in valley of dead dry bones: Valley of dry bones experience.

Eze 37: 1 – 14: The hand of the lord was on me; he brought me out by the spirit of the Lord and set in the middle of the valley; it was full of bones.

All these people were dead and dry no flesh, sinew, enzymes, intestines eyes nose. No nothing but dead and dry.

And God want to prove his ultimate power through the combination of All his power which.
1. Father God - Kratos - Yahweh
2. Son – Jesus - Ezuzia Jesus
3. Dunamis - Dunamis Holy ghost
4. Man - Intellect + All – God man

(B) THE THREE-POWER COMBINED:

1. The holy spirit = 9 gift
2. Jesus – Azuzia – kingdom accordingly gave the dead cast out devil
3. Father - Kratos

(C) GOD MAN

When God created Adam God created him in his image and after his likeness. God gave him   Dominion + Dunamis + Ezuzia + Other not yet revealed.

Man's blueprint is God almighty Yahweh – Elshaddi - Tetra gramalion.

But when man lost his glory and his relationship with God. This thing happened to Adam – Man namely:

1. Gods glory was gone
2. Ezuzia gone
3. Dumamis gone
4. Knowledge of good only gone
5. Knowledge of the word gone
6. Exceeding power gone
7. Ability to speak and plant grow not suffer gone
8. Ability to act, walk and act like God gone
9. Everything gone – lost

MANS - God glory Dimension

When man fell, he lost all the above but didn't lose everything like:

1. His intellect
2. Ability to procreate
3. Bram power
4. Physical ability
5. Science etc.

The difference is that the fall of man led to His somewhat priviedges of doing thing "with no sweat was taken away. Man must now do things with a lot of sweat involved:

Example of stuff man must do with sweat. It should have been no sweat no qualms at all but sin, sin oh sin

(E) MAN'S SWEAT - ORIGIN OF SWEAT IN LIFE

Sweat, sweating and excessive labor and laboring is a curse. This course was introduced into our world be Adam and Eve when they fell in sin. Sin will cause a man to work and work till death and achieving less. The people of the world today celebrate curses, embrace them and try to prove God. Instead come with humility and make amend and drop their sinful charter. They tend to look for ways to dry to use the other gifts they have to do without God. Humans behave like their forefathers who try to build a tower to God without his involvement.

God, we can do it without you mentally. We exist and go around without you, so that anytime you bring Gods ability and help into the equation at any level in life people will.

1. Jeer at you
2. Laugh at you
3. Blackmail you
4. Black ball you
5. Pass a vote of no confidence on you
6. Treat you like a scum
7. A religious freek
8. Estiscate themselves or avoid and isolate you.

Whereas having God in the equation is the best thing that could ever happen to man. And the most annoying part of it is that Christians are also falling for this cheap blackmail; with treat of possible imprisonment, been layed off or fired in the job, Christian compromise therefore what man could have or can possible be and also bring to the table is reduced in both quality and quantity: in both efficaly and effeconly.

GOD – MAN'S CONTRIBUTION.

1. Everything belongs to the father belong to Jesus (John 16: 15)
2. The father + son + The holy spirit belongs to us
3. The power the constellation Jesus came to them and said; *All authority in haven and on earth has been given to me* (Mt 28: 19)

THE DIFFERENCE.

When the red was divided, the Father did exceed great power Ezekiel was allowed to pertake in Gods manifestation of Kratos-Gods Almighty level.

As my father raises the dead so he has given his son also to raise the dead.

Example: The 12 yrs old girl, Jesus raises him.

Jesus was at the tomb of lasouns he prayed to the father because he was allowing the Father Jehorah to do that:

Things Jesus can do:

1. Raise certain dead
2. Heal the lame
3. Changed water to wine- John 2: 1 -11
4. Cured the noble man's son John 4: 46-47
5. The haul of fish – LK 5: 1 – 11
6. Cast out unclean sprits – Mark 1: 23 -25
7. Jesus cured Peter's Mother incur MK 1:30-31
8. Jesus healed a leper - MK 1: 40-45
9. Jesus opened eyed of blm Mt 20: 3034
10. Raise Lasains from dead

Jesus did many more miracles because the list is inexhaustible according to John 21:25 Jesus did many other things as well. If everyone of them was written down, I suppose that even the whole world would not have room for the books that would be written.

CHAPTER 9

THE HOLY SPIRIT

The holy spirit is the third person in the Trinity – The father, the son and the holy spirit – These combination beats my imagination.

The grandear the spectacular, awesome power the totality of it is more than incredible.

<u>WHO IS THE HOLY SPIRIT.</u>

Holy Spirit is

1. The breath of God.
2. Life of God

The holy spirit as Creator – Was seen when the underdeveloped word was described as "without for and VOID" and "darkness was below the depth" – GEN 1:2

And the spirit was involved in creation "hovering over the face of the waters. - Gen 1: 2

The spirit appeared first and then God started to speak. The Almighty started to speak in combination of three person using command only and sounding like one person in the Godhead or trinity speaking. One can say the holy spirit speaking until time was right and the moment was ready to create another God. Called God – Man: Then we heard introduced the "Us" and pronoun "Our"

(A) CREATION OF GOD MAN.

Gen 1: 26 – Let us create man, our image after our likeness.

This is very impressive end phensmenon in that God the father, the son and the holy spirit wanted to see the scatteved image and likeness of God which are found in three persons scattered but collected in three yet are one- together and act in unison but theses

28

whole collectibles spiritually be assembled in one man. In one person called Adam.

This is incredible and very profound. The agreement shows how

1. God is good
2. How this collective decision plays and pay better than a one man show
3. How the Lord has so much confidence in US

The God agreed to have everybody in the trinity assembled and displayed in one person Adam. But when Adam fedled he lost the glory, but God didn't change his mind. Another Adam was sent called Jesus Christ; Rom 5: 12: Therefore, as by one man sin people sinned. The world died just as by one man sin. The serpture says: Just as sin came enter into the world though one man, and death through sin and in this way, death came to all people.

So as sin entered the world though one person salvation also entered the world through one (Rom 5: 12)

So, the holy spirit has brought a lot to the table himself been the executive commander at the creation. He is not limited in the God head but unison in collective responsibility these three are united and also very good at coordinating their activities.

(B) THE GOD AGREEMENT

The God – head agreement to have the triune and only true God terbonavle terbomacled in man was not reversed, revolved or terminated because of the fall of man.

Rather, God decided to bring to the scene somebody that:

1. Restore the power
2. Make the agreement stand
3. Make everybody come back to their former state
4. Give back the glory
5. Deal with the bastard devils

HOW IT LOOKS LIKE

Jesus came into the scence as an Adam and did what the other Adam couldn't do which include:

1. Bruise the head of the serpent
2. Didn't have a compassion or wife
3. Refuse the lust of the eye
4. Refuse the loss of the flash
5. Didn't permit pride to come into his life
6. Didn't change stone to bread
7. Didn't jump from the cliff even when asked to do so
8. Didn't bow to satan when enticed by the glory of the world and riches – mammon
9. Refuse to take orders from the devil
10. Didn't make Satan of any significance at all like the world does today

HOW THE THREE GOD BEHAVE.

1. They work in cooperation with one another.
2. They work and walk in agreement.
3. They assist each other.
4. They don't disagree at all.
5. They more together and plan together.

(C) THE SYSTEM AT HAND IN THE AGREEMENT.

They have lost connection with the head; from whom the whole body supported and held together by its ligarment and sinews; grows as a God allow it to.

The whole Godhead agreed to terbancle and operate in Jesus Christ as he was on earth as a man the father was in Christ reconciling the world to himself the scripting say:

So it is Father + Son + Holy ghost + Man = God Almighty

Man, brought something to the table something positive: something wonderful and what was that:

Man brought faith to the table which satan and the demons didn't. satan taught man to sin against God. It wasn't man original intention to disobey God. But man was taught to do the untinkable that was why man's punishment was less because lucifier as a leader took advantage of man.

1. Inexperienced.
2. Nativity
3. Lack of knowledge
4. Man's unlikeness of God

And duped mankind through lie's so mans sentence was:

1. The suffering
2. Sweating and
3. Pain in childbirth by women

Dead in Christ shall rise from the dead. The father, holy spirit and Jesus will do these preachers today raise the dead today with

1. Resurrection power

CHAPTER 10

(A) OLD TESTAMENT + NEW TESTAMENT
   = Old and new
   = GODS LEVEL

Jesus combined what we are now and who we are, the Old Testament combination of both is phenomenon. Jesus said what he did, you will do also and greater works.

As Jesus was raised from the dead. With this we can do what Jesus did and what we can do.

(B) WHAT WE CAN DO

1. Time travel – When Moses was with the person 0 presence of God, he saw the past. What transpired before he was born. Moses wrote genesis and the free books God gave him the ability.

2. Translation - from Kingdom of darkness to the Kingdom of his dear son There is a gulf between the kingdom of darkness and that of light. Jesus is the only one, that could do that. Dissapparing acts like Phillip, Moses, Jesus, Ezekiel - Eze 37: 1 it is lifting in both spirit and physical.

God hates to be limited because he can do exceedingly abundantly above anybody can imagine or think.

3. Transportation – Take move people with you escape with people and you. Walking upon the water by Jesus.

4. Multiplication – multiply fish – multipler's – many things – food money etc.

   - We want the fullness, that you might be filled with the fullness of God.
   - Jesus' power is Governmental.

- The Ezuzia – governmental to human administration.
- The role of kings - subject
- The role of boss - servant
- The governmental administrative proledina in the world.
- The first Adam was a man - living soul but Jesno is a quickening spirit.

A LIVING SOUL

Gifted to operate as a man with ursden to control and organize stuff.

So, we who are human are gifted to conquer nature-built car, aeroplanes develop technology wise enjoying to do almost everything.

AS JOINT HEIRS

Rom 8: 17 Paul says "Now if we are children, then we are heirs – heirs of God and co-heirs with Christ. If indeed we share in the sufferings in order that we may also share in his glory."

If we share in his suffering will also share in his benefits.

(C) WHAT WE WILL DO IN THE GLORIOUS CHURCH

The following will be done.

1. Time travel.

2. Translation-

3. Transportation – carrying other people with you - Ezekiel resisneration of the dead solders or men took days and year later.

When Jesus will raise the whole dead people both believers & unbelievers. it will take centuries, but he will still raise everybody.

4. Multiplication - fish and fire loanes of bread multiplied to feed 5,000 men and 1,000 men excluding women and children in different occasions.

COMPARISON
PROPHETS WHO WALKED

PROPHETS WHO WALK WITH JESUS IN THE... WITH GOD IN THE...

NEW TESTAMENT	OLD TESTAMENT
Peter Shadow raises the death	**Moses** A Lot
James None I knew of	**Abraham** None I knew
John None I knew of	**Isaac** Yes
Paul A Lot	**Jacob** Yes
Jesus outstanding	**Ezekiel** A lot
Jesus raise 3 dead	**Jeremiah** A lot
Jesus open eyes of blind	**Zacharia** A lot
Phillip Disappointment	**Samson** A lot
Jesus too much and how can contain	**Joshua** jeweler walt
Peter shallow	**Skew** A lot

Kratos + Ezuzia + Dunamis = Complete level of God Almighty.

POWER OVER ELEMENTS

1. Dominion over – 5 heavens Mastery – skill to bend it to will. Bent it to you will Dominion power over it. Command it Control the time – Sun and Moon controlled.
2. WIND TO A HIGHER POWER
3. Dominion over fire and water.

The exceeding greatness of his power towards us who believe.

Testimony of how I appeared in somebody dream and told her what to do and we are tired of this status quo church setting and do something new. As children of the father, we have an inheritance with our father Jesus father, which can never spoil or perish - I Pet 1: 4

1. The people who rescue the alerted possession Jn 1: 2
2. We are his benefidiance Mt 25: 34, Gal 3: 29, Col 1: 12, 3: 24
3. Jesus the only begotten son of the father - Heb 5: 5 Ps 2: 1
4. Christ inheritance the whole world.

I NEED THE GLORY OF GOD.

What is glory of God

- Glory from the Latin gloria'' – fame renown''
- It is used to describe the manifestation of god's presence as percussed by humans according to the Abrahamic religious.

The glory of God is the beauty of his spirit. It is not an aesthetic beauty or a material beauty, but it is the beauty that emanates from God Almighty.

DOMMON AND MASTERY OPEN THE TRUE ELEMENT.

1 Land – God starts with dirt, mountain

Mountain – whole land masses not just troubles – God command the land to come out of the water and:

1. Let snakes come out,
2. Grasses
3. Jesus spat on dirt and amointed the man eyes. Mastery over dirt to do miracles.

Ascenders - He descend first before ascending

Descenders- Going into hell and been shown things there.

Movers – Global Ministry.

Say to this mountain be how removed.

Connection to strong faith though spoken words.

Shakers – Ability to transform below those who have physical power to shack.

1. Jesus' reassertion led to earthquake
2. When God came on mont SINIA, there was both lypobolic and physical shakening EA Ade-

Invisibleness - Exceeding greatness of his power toward us.

1. He walks too walls
2. Disappear
3. Re-appear
4. Sufferings and glory.

He is over all things whether invisible or visible.

Invisible things are read.

1. Small
2. Eyes cannot see them
3. Need optical enhancement.

WHY THE INVISIBLENESS

1. To save his work
2. To save his child.

Example:

1. Uma UKPai trip to China and the bible in the frunk but invicible to the police.
2. My friend with a contribel in his purse mistakenly kept their and the police didn't see.

Read Ocean deal for full story: The father of our Lord Jesus Christ, gave us the ability to pray the God of our Lord Jesus is Jehovbi

WHO ARE GODS MENTIONED IN THE BIBLE.

1. The father – as God
2. The Holy spirit – as God
3. Jesus as God – as God
4. Man as God
5. Satan as God

6. Moses as God

But there is not any other God beside the Almighty.

WHAT WE ARE BECOMING AND HIS CALLING.

1. Hope of his calling
2. Riches of glory of his inheritance
3. Exceeding greatness of his power of the ressuction from the dead.

Power - Kartoos

This power of Kartos is given to us so we can also need wisdom to be trained to understand the exceeding greatness of his power.

They have a form of godliness and denying the power thereof.

Also, God gives people this man lent not until after a certain. They were put before tutors until the day of...

Nothing is limiting with God.

IGNORING THE FATHER

You will not ask me anything

You will go to the father

1. We ought to Jehorah God
2. We need to talk and relate with the father
3. When we receive the father, we receive Kratos

Ph 1: 15

*The God of our father Je*sus.

Also, to many:
Touch me not for I have not yet ascended unto the father.

In the garden of Gethsemane:

Jesus got on his knees and prayed to the father.

Para – bole – Paragraph – Paracletes - comforter- helper

Father, son & Holy spirit.

Jn 14: 16, 26, Jn 15: 26

Lk 3: 22 – All there at the same conversation – Time wonderful, You're wonderful.

Act 5: 3

- You need rude awakening.

CHAPTER 11

GOD THE HOLY SPIRIT

INTRODUCTION

<u>JOHN 14:</u>

He is at the upper nontalking to his disciples

JOHN 14: 31

Jesus said let us go

JOHN 14, 16 – 17

I will pray the father and he will give you another Helper

Pray – ask

He – Means the holy spirit is a He and He is used because

1. We can develop a personal relationship with him
2. We can speak with him
3. Communicate and he can also speak back to us

WHO IS THE HOLY SPIRIT

-Is the third person in the God – Head - The father, the son and the Holy spirit the bible will say.

<u>John 14: 25 – 27</u>

The Helper

<u>John 15: 26</u>

When the achogate comes
Whom I will send to you from the faith

<u>John 16: 7 – 8 – 1 1-1</u>

I will send them to you

<u>John 16: 12</u>

What belongs to the father is mine.
The is I said the spirit wiil ...

Emphasis on WORD

1. Helper - Paracletes - Comforter

(A) WHO IS THE HOLY SPIRIT (What does he do)
How the Holy Spirit He

Jn 16: 8

He is going to connect the world
Vs g: of (1) Sin because they do not believe me.
The holy spirit convinces or convicts us of the need of Jesus Christ. His blood

Jn 16: 10

Convict or convince us of Righteousness.
(A) Right standing with and live righteously

Vs 11

The holy spirit convicts us of judgment
Because the devil is judged.

Jn 12: 31

Jn 14: 30

(2) Holy spirit is our friend He is nice happy and nice. He is not SPOOKY.
He is not mean

Mathew 12: 32b

Anyone who speaks word against the holy spirit will not be forgiven either in this age or in the age to come.

People are scared of this passage and other passages in the scripture as
A. Stricker than the rest in the God head.
B. Holy spirit as the father
C. The one that slays – "Slain" in the spirit
D. Convicted – Prosecuted by the spirit or
E. Judgmental spirit

But that is not the case. The holy spirit is as sweet as the father caring and nice.

Remember the fruits of the holy spirit's name: Kindness, goodness, gentleness, long suffering, LOVE, etc.

All these explain the person of the holy spirit. So, there is nothing spooky, wired, eerie, uncanny, unnaturally unnatural about the acts of the holy spirit.

(B) THE WORLD VIEW OF THE HOLY SPIRIT

1. Preternatural
2. Supernatural
3. Unearthly ghostly
4. Other worldly
5. Mysterious
6. Mystifying
7. Strange
8. Strange
9. Freaky
10. Rum

In addressing this topic, the world may be right about some of their assumption especially when it come to the manifestation of the power and the display of them. The bible is full of these heart renching, earth shaking, ground moving, heavy noise and other really weird displays: Like

1. Act 2: 2
When the day of Pentecost
Was fully come...................

All theses manifestations is to announce the coming of our Lord holy ghost to the scene – The some, the noise as mighty rusling word etc. All can be really ''Spooky'' if you like but.

1. That is one of the ways he announces his entrants.
2. He comes sometimes as gently rain
3. A still small voice
4. Like a dew.

(C) WHAT I DON'T WANT TO DO.

1. I don't want to write and lie that its not sometimes very supernatural.
2. I don't want to take away the gradeur and fantastic entry into the scene by the holy spirit.
3. I am not going to say it is normal.
4. Not ordinary
5. The world cannot receive him some of the teachings and lectures and semim about the holy spirit has ''Induce a sence of disbelief or alienation in people about the good person of the holy ghost.

1. The Old Testament depict the holy spirit as coming upon people and they do mighty stuff like Samson and the holy spirit comes and go like a ''blue eyed immigrant God that ''comes from heaven and go back there after causing, tornadoe, death famine and other natural disaster.
2. THE NEW TESTAMENT. But the same preachers claim, Jesus is so nice '' gentle Jesus Meek and Mild'' they say in songs, poetry, traditional folk love etc.
3. The combination of both old and New Testament which is the Bible explains that all these three are
   1. United in purpose.
   2. Organized and operation.
   3. Dependable in judgment. In short, they are one.

Nothing creepy about the Holy Spirit but to unbeliever. He can be very supernatural and scary.

Satan created a lot of carturence by causing confusion by put our focus on one God – Jesus

(D) EVIDENCE:
a. Power to witness
b. Fruits of the spirit
c. Love
d. Gifts = 9

1. Friend
2. God's partners
3. Negatives of the Holy Spirit

1. If I mention father and you are comfortable
2. If I mention the Lord Jesus and you are cool
3. If I mention the holy spirit and freak out some things wrong somewhere. Jesus God & Holy Spirit and the Father in one scripture.

<u>John 14: 16 – 14: 26</u>

<u>Jn 25: 26</u>

Lk 3: 22 – *The holy spirit descended in bodily form*
The father glorifies, Jesus and then Jesus does only
Two scripture that says the holy is God

Act 5: 23 – 4
GOD WE NEVER KNEW

Is He Real.

CHAPTER 12

THE FULLNESS OF GOD's GLORY MANIFESTATION

Joel 2: 28: And it shall come to pass afterward; that I will pour out my spirit all flash and your sons and your daughters shall prophesy, your old men chean dreams, your young man shall see visions.

This was a promise from God to the people. Straight from God to reassure the people of his hope for their calling to be servants of God. Worshipper like their fore-father Abraham, Isaac and Jacob. More so, it is a promise to the patriechs about their future. God was assuming them through prophet, Joel of his faith fullness Don't give up he said.

God has many spirits.

Depiction of the family

<u>Jn 15: 16</u>
said the holy from the father

<u>Rev 4: 5</u>
Symbol as seen

<u>Zac 4: 2</u>
Solid gold lamb stand

<u>Rev 5: 2 - 6</u>
Seven eyes of the lamb omnpersence of God

<u>Rev 5:</u>
6seven eyes of the lamb ommenous-omnopersence
Seven spirits symbolies the holy spirit.

(A) SIGNIFICANCE OF # 7

1. Perfection – completeness
   Isaac 11: 2 – Seven complete
   Not seven individual spirits but combination of 7
2. Thus, the Isiah 11: 2
   a. The spirit of wisdom
   b. Spirit of understanding
   c. Counsel 4 power 5 knowledge
   d. Knowledge of God (7) fear of God
   One spirit described in seven ways.

(B) THE MANY SPIRITS OF GOD

There are many spirits of God. These Spirit are known and mentioned in the bible. They are either mentioned collectively or given individual manifestation and nor menctature.

We shall look at the following:
- The seven spirits of God
- Isiah 11: 1 – 3
- Including the spirit of the Lord, and the spirit of wisdom, of understanding

1. Rev 1: 4 – 5: *John to the seven churches in the promise of Asia. Grace and peace to you from Him who is, who was and who is to come, and from the seven spirits..............*
2. Rev 3: 1 – *To the angel of the church in said is write "These are the word of him who hold the seven spirits of God.*
3. Rev 4: 5 – *From the throne came flashes of lighterings, rumblings and peals of thunder in front of the throne. Seven lambs were blazing. These are the seven spirits of God.*
4. Rev 5: 6 – *"There I saw a lam looking like as if it I had been slam..............*

The lamb had seven horse and seven eyes which are the seven spirits of God.

The identity of these seven spirits do not see explicit but can be explained. It cannot be the presence of anngelie being such as cherubim or seraphim.

Jn 1: 4 - 5: Relief is coming from
1) ...
2) seven spirits
3) from Jesus Christ.

(C) THE SEVEN SPIRIT AS TRINITY.

The seven spirit appears to be both

1. Personality and characteristics of the Triune God -The father Son and the holy spirit explain as seven but still one individual God.
2. The seven spirits as offices of the true Gods – In one God Almighty.
3. As their allubutes combined in to one but can separated.
4. As thrones – horn
5. Eyes connections and what they see how and judgment.
6. What they give and do to the world. As people receive God they become clothe with this spirit.
7. And truly the spirit is unique and specific.
8. Can be separated and also, they can be concentrated in one person

In Rev: 3: 1 – *"Jesus holds the seven spirits of God.*

In John 15: 26: *Jesus sends you the holy spirit from the father passage kind of suggest.*

a. Super ordinate

b. Subordinate, cadre strata or organa gram relationship while in reclamation Rev 4: 5 – The seven spirits of God are symbolized as seven burning lamps that are before God's throne. These can also be seven in the book of Zacharia: '' Zachariah's vision'' which he said the holy spirit symbolized as'' a solid gold lamp stand—with a bowl at the top and seven lamps on it (Zac 4: 2)

Whole in Rev 5: 6 - *The seven spirits of the lamb are the seven eyes sent out into all the world.*

These 7 eyes speak of the spirit and the lamb together supervised and overseen by the father. The three persons these speaks of the ommpresence and omniscient of God. The three together.

Once we identify the whole" seven spirits as the holy spirit" i.e 7 in one spirit. Then we can go ahead and bring them together as still part of the lamb and the father

CHAPTER 13

(A) WHAT IT LOOKS LIKE
1. Holy spirit 7- spirit
2. 7 Spirit - Holy spirit
3. Eyes - Holy spirit ---- investigation into gathering
4. Horns - Holy spirit with thrones
5. Eyes sent - Omni presents
6. Horns - Government on Jesus, father, and Holy spirit. spirit of wisdom
7. Spirit of wisdom
8. Spirit of the Lord
9. Spirit of understanding
10. Spirit of counsel
11. Spirit of power.
12. Sprit of knowledge
13. Spirit of the fear of God.

So, we can say that the" seven spirits of God"in the book of revelation are thus a reference to the Holy Spirit and ministry on earth and in heaven.

THE POWER OF THE HOLY SPIRIT.

The holy spirit power sometimes called the ''holy ghost power'' is the power which sometimes   reflects in the natural as well as the superrelvant. He gives us, Power, Love and sound mind.

Self discipline and peace – Holiness and righteousness.

Power can mean many things to many people. But power backed with the holy spirit or by the holy will be:
1. Pure
2. According to Gods plan.

3. Supported by all the God head
4. Assisted by all God head together.
   Check this out
   If the spirit that raise
   Jesus from the dead.

(B) SIX WAYS THE HOLY SPIRIT TRANSFORM OUR LIVES

1. Make us more like Christ
2. He gives us power to witness
3. Guides us into all truth
4. The holy spirit convicts us of sin.
5. The holy spirit reveals Gods word to us
6. The holy spirit brings us closer to other believers.

OTHER THINGS THE HOLY SPIRIT.
1. RAISE THE DEAD
2. HEAL THE SICK
3. OPEN THE EYES OF BLIND.
4. TRUN WATER TO WINE
5. CLENSE LEPROSY

In fact, everything wonderful manifestation or good deals done or know to be done by Jesus and the father were done in conjuction or coalition with the holy ghost period.

(C) WHAT THE HOLY SPIRIT DID FOR US.

1. Gen 11: 1 Tower of Babel
   (A) They spoke one language confused them
   (B) They gather in pride Pentecost:
2. They came together Pentecost is blessed river sail of the course of God.
   Law given - Lord noise, colored discribel 3000 dead

Pentecost - Fire, cloud descended, God wrote his law on men's he rent, and 3000 men Saved.

(C) Day of Pentecost

- is a fulfillment of God promised Messiah and the holy ghost coming to enable us to make it.

The holy spirit comes to empower us to work righteously. Can we experience Pentecost today.

Act 2: 3 - Divided tongues.

1. Yes, we can – Individual tonge as of fire
2. Satan deal of them
3. Other languages come to them
4. People gathered were shocked when the earth moved due to Holy Spirit manifestation.
5. Power to witness
6. Power to preach came up on Peter.

Can I receive the holy spirit

Act 1: 4 – 5

Act 2: 38 – After Peter the timid apostle receved the holy spirit he was energized to preach. And the people asked the fundamental question Act 2: 38 – 39

Act 2: 38 - 39 - Peter replied, repart and be baptized everyone of you, in the name of Jesus Christ for the forgiveness of your sins, and you will receive the gift of the holy spirit.

(E) HOLY SPIRIT COMMON OR POPULAR

DOES HE BAPTIZE
1 COR 10: 5 - baptism in the holy spirit
  1. The holy spirit baptizes us into Christ Jesus body.

1 COR 10: 15 - Baptism from the Greek word buptiso.
Mt 28: 19 - Baptism in water. We can see the unity of the father the son and the holy ghost here again.

Baptism
Eph 4:
  One baptism –
  And one Lord –

Three in heaven which agree and on earth that agree. Jesus baptizes in the holy spirit.

Mt 3: 11: ''Indeed I baptize John was not speeky of the to the 12 dneysles or the 120 people in the upen room John was referring to Jesus' discipline in John chapter 3 because Jesus hadn't called his disciples yet but John was referring to Jesus. Jesus called his disciples John.

CHAPTER 14

1. The holy = 1 Cor 12: 13
2. The disciples = Mt 28: 13
3. Jesus baptizes = Mt 3: 11
   Mk 1: 8 John 1: 33
   1K 3: 16

(A) SALVATION, WATER AND SPIRIT.

- Salvation - born again as perfect
- Children of God – Col 3: 6
- Jesus was born perfect so didn't need to be born again.
- Was Jesus water baptized?
  - Yes, Jesus was baptized in water by John as the Jordan river it is considered to have taken place at Al-Maqhtas, also called Bethany, Beyond the Jordan.
- Was Jesus spirit baptized?
  - Yes Jesus was spirit baptized after his water baptism by John the baptizer:

UNDERSTANDING THE TEXT
Mathew records that when Jesus asked John to baptize him, John was reluctant to do so due to the fact that
1. Baptism by water is for sinner which Jesus became. - He was not but he became due to his hot love for the father and us. However, he became sin and need baptism, but John didn't know all the complete information which is what I call "Spiritual conjecture"
2. Jesus the greater person:
3. The father had programmed it to be sow
4. All the scripture must be fulfilled

WAS JESUS SPIRITUALLY BAPTIZED?

Yes, Jesus was spiritually baptized. The bible says at the moment Jesus came out of river Jordam, Jesus was also immediately and histataously baptized in the holy ghost or with the holy ghost or both and the follow significant events occurred.

1. Heaven was opened.
2. God's spirit descended on him like a dove.
3. God's voice was heard like thunder
4. God actually endorsed Jesus ''by saying this is my beloved son in whom I am well pleased''

The Dove is always simbolie of the holy spirit then; also represent peace.

(A) This confirms Jesus' endorsement by the holy spirit.

(B) Gods voice heard and what he said furthermore confirms Jesus

IDENTITY AS THE SON OF GOD.

The crowd of the people at the bank of the river heard it Peter made reference to it when they were about to choose.

Which of the disciples fit to replace Judas Iscariot who was dead.

Peter said: The new apostle to be selected must be one of the disciples who had been with from thedisciples who had been with from the baptism of Jesus at the Jordan till his death and resurrection. And they last lot on these qualified and the lot fell on Matthias.

QUESTION

If Jesus needed the holy spirit and how much more do you think of the holy do you need.

Act 8: 12 - 14

Act 8: 15 - Prayed for them to receive the holy spirit.

Act 19: 1 - Despite Apollos preaching, they didn't receive the holy because Apollos didn't know of the baptism of the holy ghost.

There you receive the holy spirit.

We don't know of the existence of the holy spirit.

1. He then baptized him with water

2. After they were baptized in the holy ghost

1. Act 8 – 5yrs after Pentecost
2. Act 10 – 10 yrs later – Gentiles were bap
3. Act 19 – 25 yrs after Pentecost

Did you receive the holy spirit when you
1. 1 JN 5: 7: Trinity =
2. The three baptisms of Holy Spirit:

1. 1 John 5: 8
2. 1 Cor 10: 1

Moses was Israel's type of deliver an example or symbol of the new by the holy spirit.

PROCESS BEFORE BAPTISM.

- Blood
- Holy
- Holy Place
- Holy Water
- Oil
- Flask

Entry into the terbanele requires 3 baptisms or 3 things to do:
1. Alter - where the blood of the levls is shared = Salvation.
2. Laver - water
3. Flask - Amounted with oil

Some people Christians don't want to fulfill all the protocol or process and want to circumvent the process and go into the holy place and into the holy of holiest. And what happens.

WHEN WE JUMP THE PROCESS, WE DIE.

That is what happens to people who think they can set the rules.

You don't have to set the rules. Jesus is the one that anoint us in the spirit, with the spirit.

When you receive Jesus, you are qualified to receive the Holy Spirit. And you can receive that Holy Spirit as you read this book.

The Holy Spirit loves you and eager to help you, enter you and stay with you. The father, the son and the holy spirit want to gee with you and make their dwelling with you.

God is more excited than us

John 14: 23

Jesus answered and said into him, if love me, he will keep my words, and my father will love him; and

We will come unto him and make our abode with him.

Jesus is the holy spirit, father and holy spirit, they are one.

In this study of the cadre of the Godhead is symbolic of the unity expected of us along side the trinity.

CONCLUSION

In conclusion the: Father, the son and the holy spirit are one.

In the Cadre or orgamagram of God everybody is important in the decision-making process.

These is significant because in the creation Gen 1: - The holy spirit appeared in the scene, then the

Holy spirit did his own, the father took over and started speaking: '' Let there be'', let there be''

This and that:

From Genesis to revelations there has been together, united and one. We too are united with them

We are together and in one with the God head.

Our entry point was through Jesus Christ, and this made us joint heirs with Christ and automatically made us inclusive of everything. We have a very strong coverant with all the trinity though Jesus Christ.

We are not only connected to Christ as understood by some people.

The Jews claim only God the father. The Christians claim only God the son and a few accept the holy spirit or holy ghost.

But the truth is that; we Christians need to know the father Jews or Judaism follow need to embrace Jesus Christ and the holy spirit to be complete in Christ in God.

To avoid spiritual conjecture, we need the baptism of the 3 God Cadre or realm.

I want to enjoin my readers to buy this book for their friends, family and co-workers it will be a good gift.

God bless you all.